With all my love to Eyan, Aariyan and Mischa.

...and to all the children whose lives have been forever impacted by the COVID-19

Excited about his playdate with his older cousin Ella, Milo ran to the playground but when he saw Ella, Milo came to a screeching halt. Ella was wearing something on her face that covered her mouth and nose.

What's that on your face, Milo asked.

It's a mask, Ella said.

A mask?!?...like what superheroes wear?!, Milo asked.

Ella laughed and said, 'No, this mask just covers your mouth and nose'.

I thought it would be a good idea to talk about germs while we played today and how we can protect each other from some pretty nasty ones out there, Ella said.

GERMS?! What are germs? Milo asked.

Germs are everywhere. They are small organisms. Ella said.

ORGA-WHAT?!?, yelled Milo.

Organisms! They are living things. And germs are small, sneaky organisms that

can creep into your body and make you sick, Ella said.

Eewww….BLECH!

germs sound gross, Milo exclaimed.

Ella continued explaining, germs are everywhere and on everything. For instance, germs are in the air, they are on other people, they are on these swings and now they are on your hands from touching these swings, Ella said.

In the air and on everything??!,

Eewww, DISGUSTING!

Time To Wear a Mask,

exclaimed Milo.

If germs are everywhere and on everything, do you always have to wear a mask, asked Milo

Good question, Ella said. I think it
depends on what works best for
you, your brother, and your mommy
and daddy. And that may be
different from what works best for
your friends and their family. The
important thing to remember is
that we all do what we can to
protect each other from getting
sick. Covering your mouth when
you cough or sneeze can also
prevent you from spreading germs.
Another way to prevent spreading
germs is to keep your distance
from others when you're sick.

I like those ideas, Milo said as he
tried on a mask.

Now that you know how to protect your mouth and nose from germs in the air, do you know what to do about those dirty hands?, asked Ella.

Eewww, Time To Wash Our Hands, exclaimed Milo.

That's exactly right, Milo. Washing your hands is the best way to prevent spreading germs, Ella said.

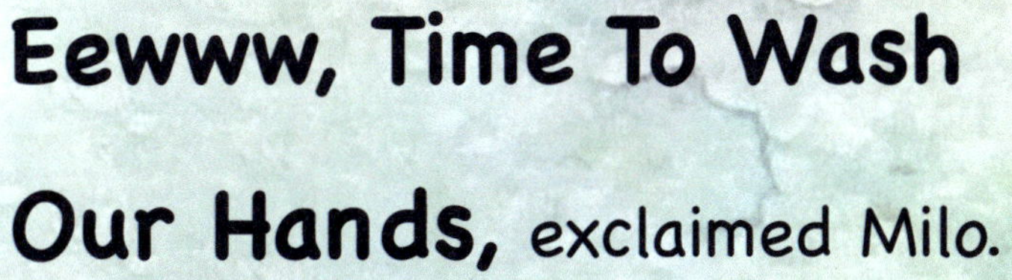

Do you know how to wash your hands properly, Ella asked Milo.

Yes, Milo said, I know that one!
You wash your hands with soap
while singing the ABCs.

That's right, Ella said. Remember
Milo, it's really important to rub
your hands together and make
sure you wash in between your
fingers too.

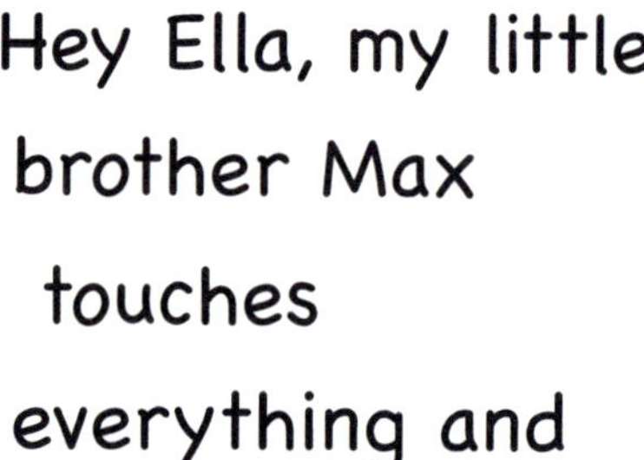

Hey Ella, my little brother Max touches everything and sometimes puts things in his mouth. Do you think he should learn about germs too, Milo asked.

Yes, Ella said, I don't think its ever too early to learn about germs.

Let's go and tell him before he puts another thing in his mouth, Milo said.

Though young, Max was shocked
to hear what Ella and Milo had to
say about germs. When Max was
all done learning about germs,
they all agreed,

Eewww, Yucky Germs!!!

Before Ella went home, she told Milo what a great job he did learning about germs. Milo was sad to say good bye to Ella but he knew that Ella would be back soon. Milo always enjoyed learning from his older cousin. She made everything so much fun...even learning!

Activity Pages

Coloring Page

Coloring Page

Coloring Page

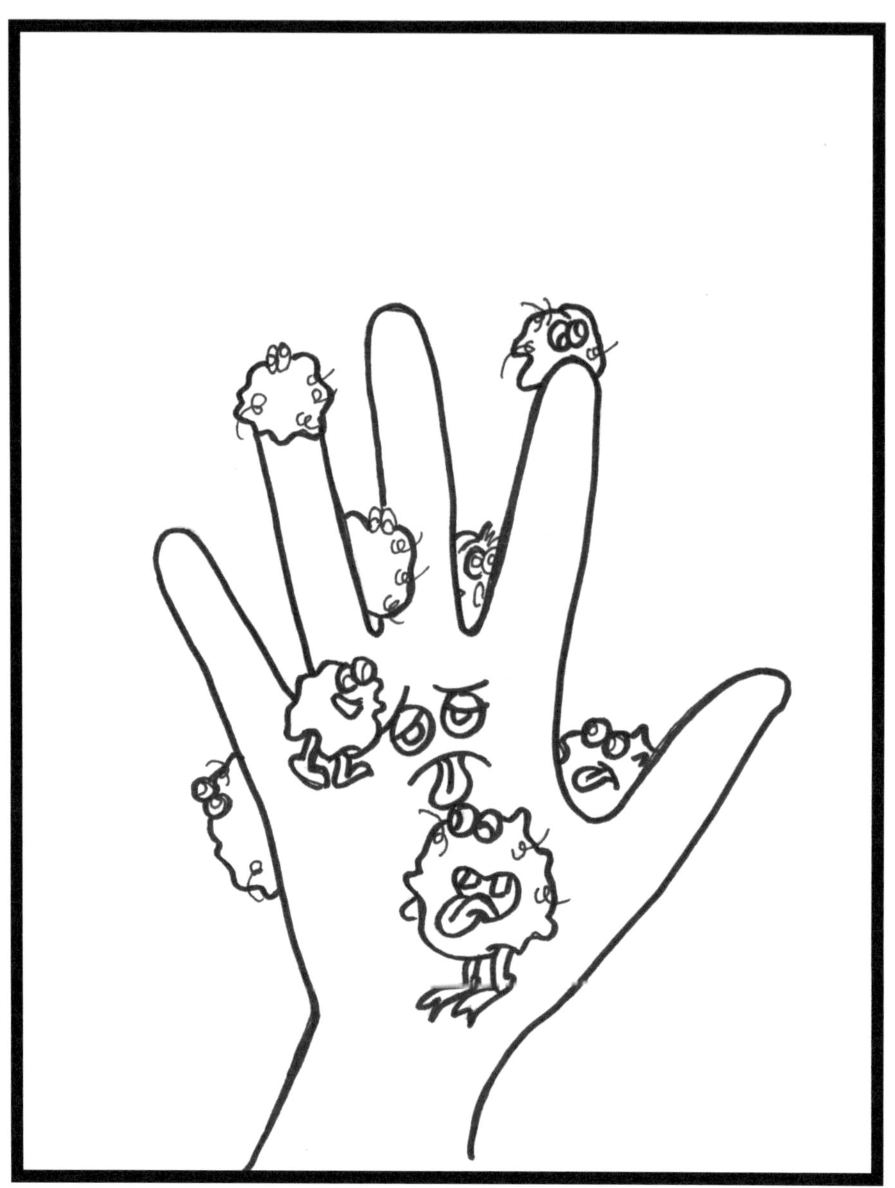

Coloring Page

Coloring Page

Coloring Page

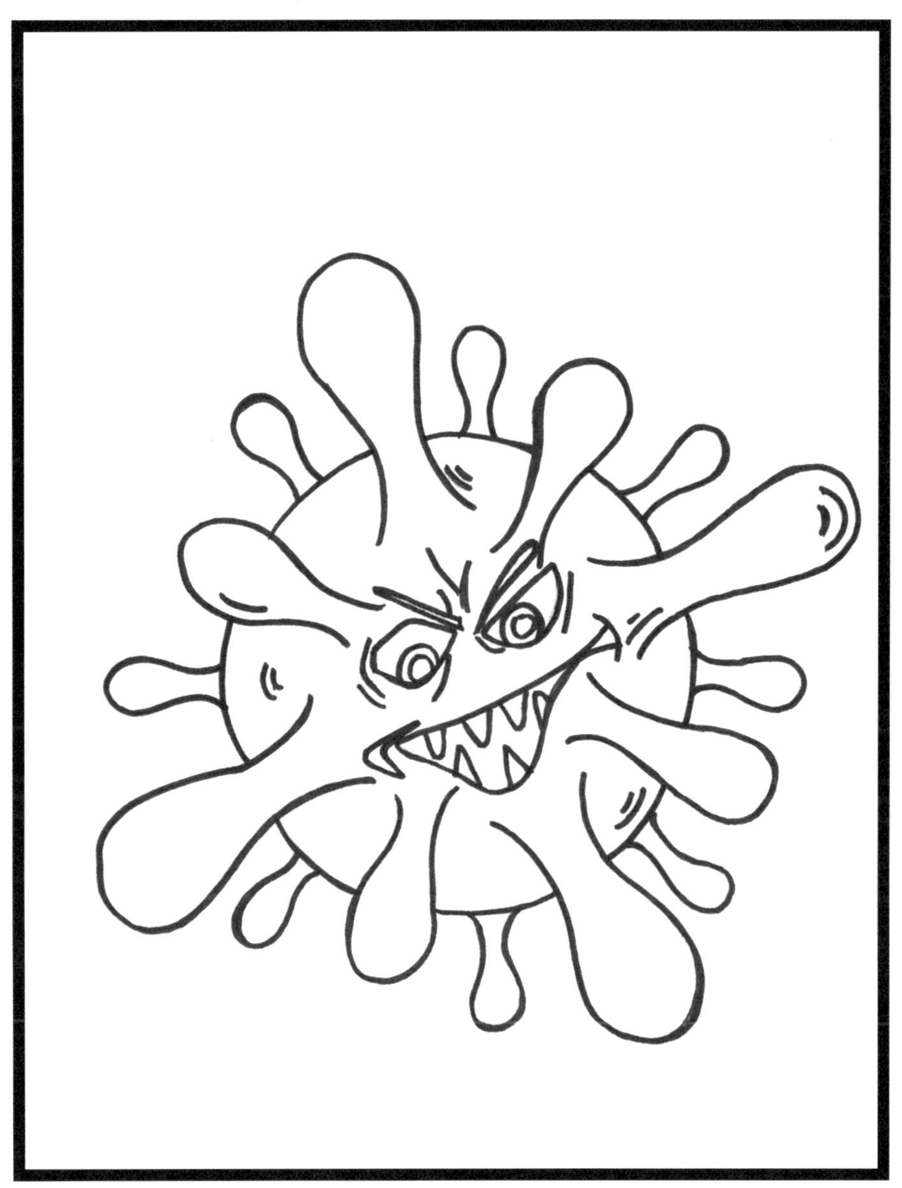

REVEAL THE HIDDEN MESSAGE

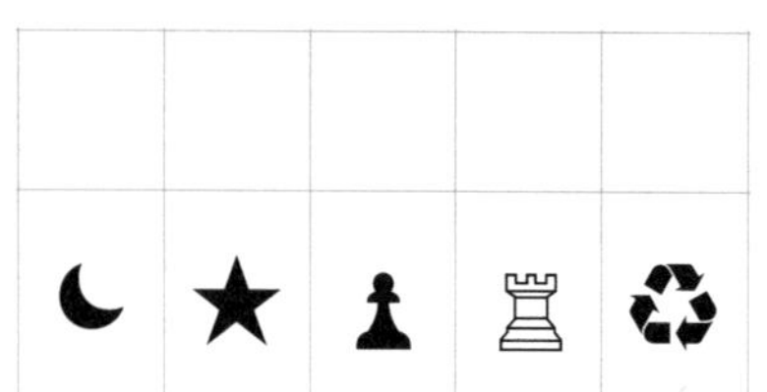

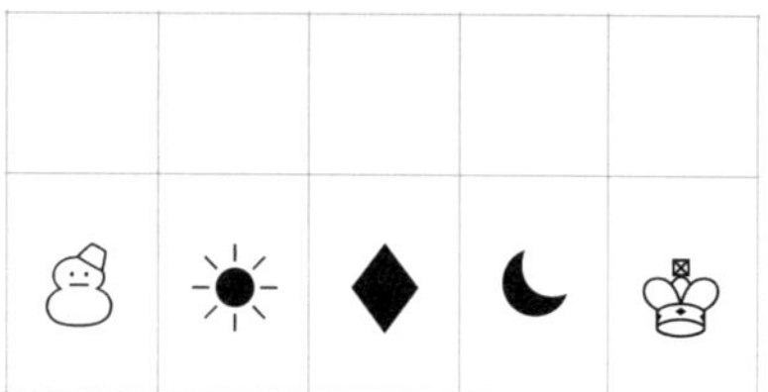

Key

Made in the USA
Monee, IL
07 July 2026

56551698R00017